All rights reserved

- Copyright © 2017 Katarina Garnett
- Naturally Richer
- **www.naturallyricher.com**
- naturallyricher@gmail.com
- **ISBN   978 – 80 – 973 149 – 1 – 0**

- Author Katarina Garnett
- Edited by Leila, David and Emma Garnett   Thank you

This book belongs to

I dedicate this book
to my girls
Leila and Evinia,
who are the greatest
inspiration
in my life.

Thank you.

WORDS OF NATURE

ARA
MACAW

This book is part of a series

Love Learn Leave

In this book Max, the Macaw,
will take you into his world.

He will tell you all about himself and his friends.

You will find out where he lives, what he eats,
how he nests and many more things about him.

He will also tell you how his world is threatened
and how you can help him.

A simple yet strong message....

There is of huge importance to understand and realize,
that we, humans, are just a part of a huge living organism.

We are cutting down trees
and forest like there is no tomorrow....
Polluting rivers and oceans,
poisoning the soil and our food.

We do not see how many living beings we destroy.
Or how we damage ecosystems, how we hurt animals
and even each other....

Many people pretend, that animals do not have feelings.
They say, that they do not feel pain the way we do
and that nature and animals are here to serve people.

It is Ok they say, they are just animals....

We need to realize, that Nature
is what we need the most.
There is no tomorrow without nature.
There is no us without nature....

Nature means plants and animals living
in harmony together....

Nature doesn't need us,
we need Nature.

To be inspired is great, to inspire is incredible....

Hi there. How are you?
My name is Max. I am a bird, a parrot.
I'm also called a Green Wing Macaw, or Ara,
the third largest of all Macaws.

I am 6 years old and I will live to be 60 or more.

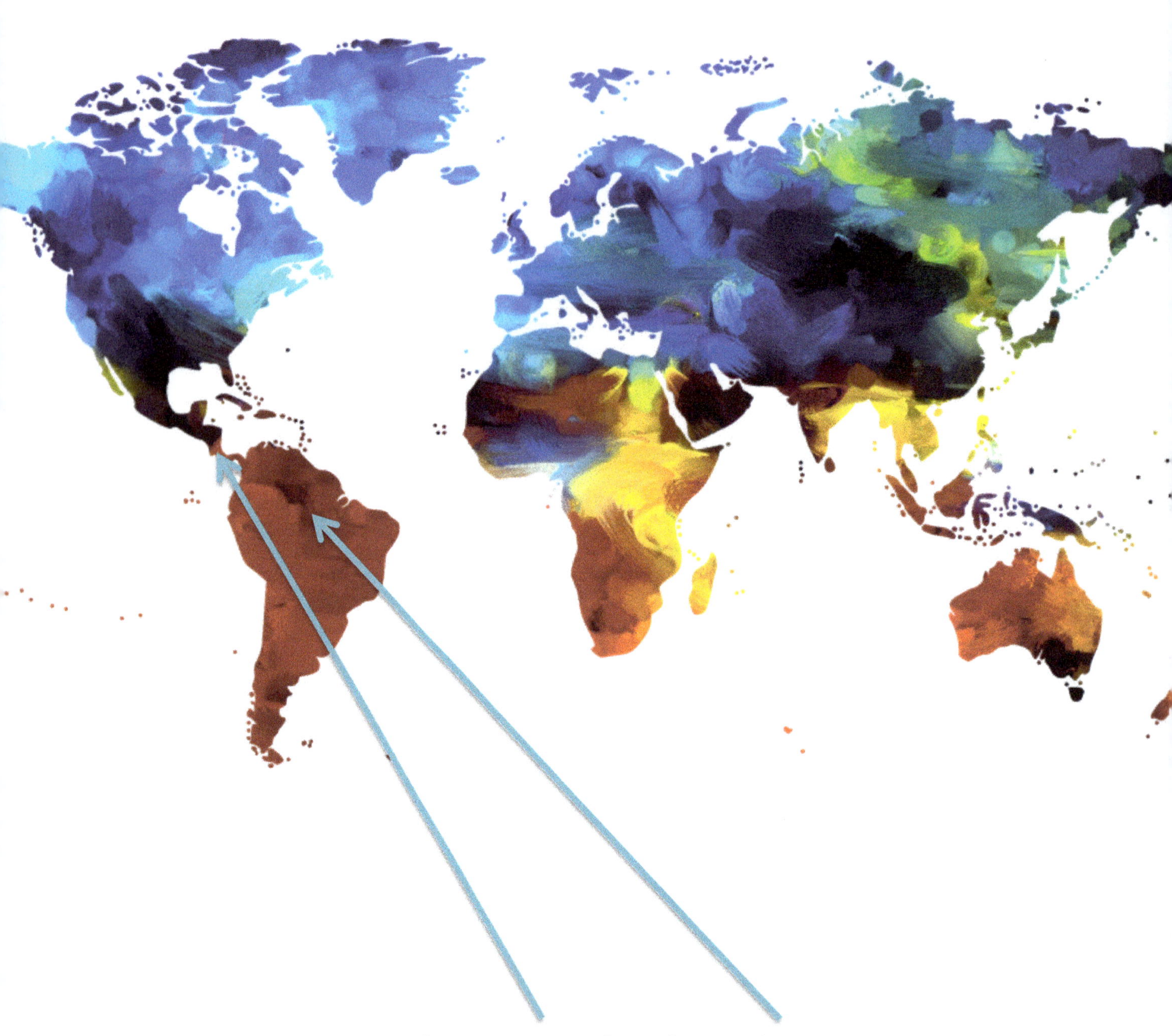

I come from Central and South America.

You can find me anywhere between
Southern Mexico and Northern Argentina.

Some macaws prefer **rainforests**, some savannas
and some woodland habitats.

I live in a tropical rainforest, which is a very special place.
It has a warm and wet climate and it is also called a **jungle**.
Trees here never lose their leaves.

More than half of the worlds animals and plants live here.
Many of them, people haven't even seen yet.

People use many natural remedies
from this amazing **ecosystem.**

(**Ecosystem** – a community of organisms,
living together in their shared environment)

There are few undisturbed rainforests left around the world.
They are very important for animals, plants,
but also for people.

Have you ever been in a rainforest?

What about you?
Where do you live?

I share my home with leopards, snakes,
sloths and thousands of other animals too....

Did you know that there are at least
17 species of Macaws living in the wild?

We all differ in size and colour.

Even within the same species,
there are no two Macaws, that are exactly the same.

Our facial pattern is as unique as your fingerprint.

We, Macaws,
are also the biggest parrot species.

You can see how big we are in comparison
to some of our smaller cousins....

We live in flocks,
but when we are raising our young,
we stay with our mate.
A mate that we
choose for life.

We make nests in tree
hollows that are big enough
for us.

Just like some other birds do.

The male Macaw forages for food, while the female
stays in the nest and incubates the eggs.
We also share food with our mate.

And we will feed our young
with pre - chewed food,
like this…

My foot has four toes that help me to hold my food
and examine new and interesting things.

The first and fourth toe always point backward.

The other two are pointed forward.

They help me to balance and hold on
to the branches of the trees.

I can always count on my feet for a safe landing
after flight.

Look how I can hold
this nut in my foot.

Can you do this too?

See how I crack it
with my sharp beak?

It's very tasty.

Do you like nuts ?

I love to eat seeds,
fruits, greens, flowers ,
nuts and stems.

Sometimes I have to eat
clay – soil, to clear my
body of harmful toxins.

Did you know, that I have a bone in my tongue?

It helps me to get the food from difficult places, or examine things that I am interested in.

It's like having a finger in your mouth.

Handy tool isn't it?

I love to play around.
There are so many places to hide here
in the rainforest.

PEAK-A-BOO!

Amy plays with me too.

Do you like to play hide and seek?

I have so many friends here.
Let me show you some of them;
This is Evi.
She sings all day long.
She is a Hyacinth - blue Macaw.
The biggest Macaw of us all.
From the top of her head to the tip of her tail
she measures up to 1 meter long.

Leo is very nosy.

He wants to know everything!

And he can't keep any secrets either...!

Betty and Ruby are lovely ladies.
They always tell us stories...
stories that have been passed down
for many generations.
Important knowledge about us and our home.

Ruby

Tony is a Great Green
Macaw.

He is very clever
and very big.

The second biggest
of all the Macaws.

His kind have become
very rare....

Sam loves to play
with sticks.

He always comes up
with new tricks.

Leila is very
colourful and very
kind.

She is also
6 years old.
Just like me.

Katie is my best friend.
She is a Scarlet Macaw
Together we love to explore new places and meet new bird species.
There are so many of them out there.
More than all of my feathers put together.

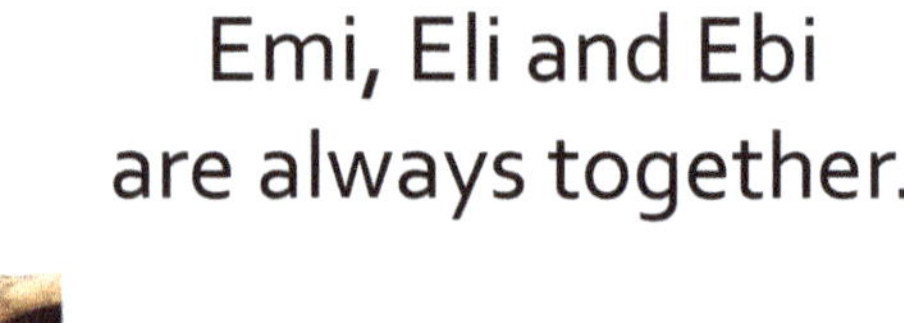

Emi, Eli and Ebi
are always together.

They are
Blue - Yellow Macaws.

Just like the sun in the blue
sky.

These Macaws are old and wise.

They relax and always
take their time.

Rozy, Hozy, Mozy and Fozy
are their names.

Dave is a big dreamer.

There are no limits in his world.

Forever hungry Luca has his eyes
on some tasty fruit....

Soon, he will be so heavy,
that he won't be able to fly.

My friend's feathers have the most amazing colours.

Some are red and orange, some yellow and green,
some blue, indigo and violet too.

Just like the rainbow.

Look how colourful our feathers can be.

How many colours can you see?

Can you count them all?

How many did you find?

And what about here?

On our wings, we have feathers long and short....

They are all very important.

They help us fly
high above the ground.

Just like this...

Our very long tail
has it's purpose
too.

It helps us land, perch, turn
in flight, slow down
and take off.

And that is why we need to take
good care of all our feathers and keep
them healthy and clean.

Most of the time we do it ourselves....

But sometimes we get a little help
from our friends....

A quick shower and our feathers are good as new….

The natural world is beautiful after a rainy day too….

Some of us are not so lucky and cannot fly free.
People have taken many chicks out of our nests.
They take them from our families and send them far away
to pet shops, where people can buy them as their pets.

They want to keep them at home in cages
which are often very small.
Many of them have to learn and perform
all kinds of tricks....

Some are so unhappy there, that they will
pluck their own feathers out.
(**Pluck** – pull out feathers)

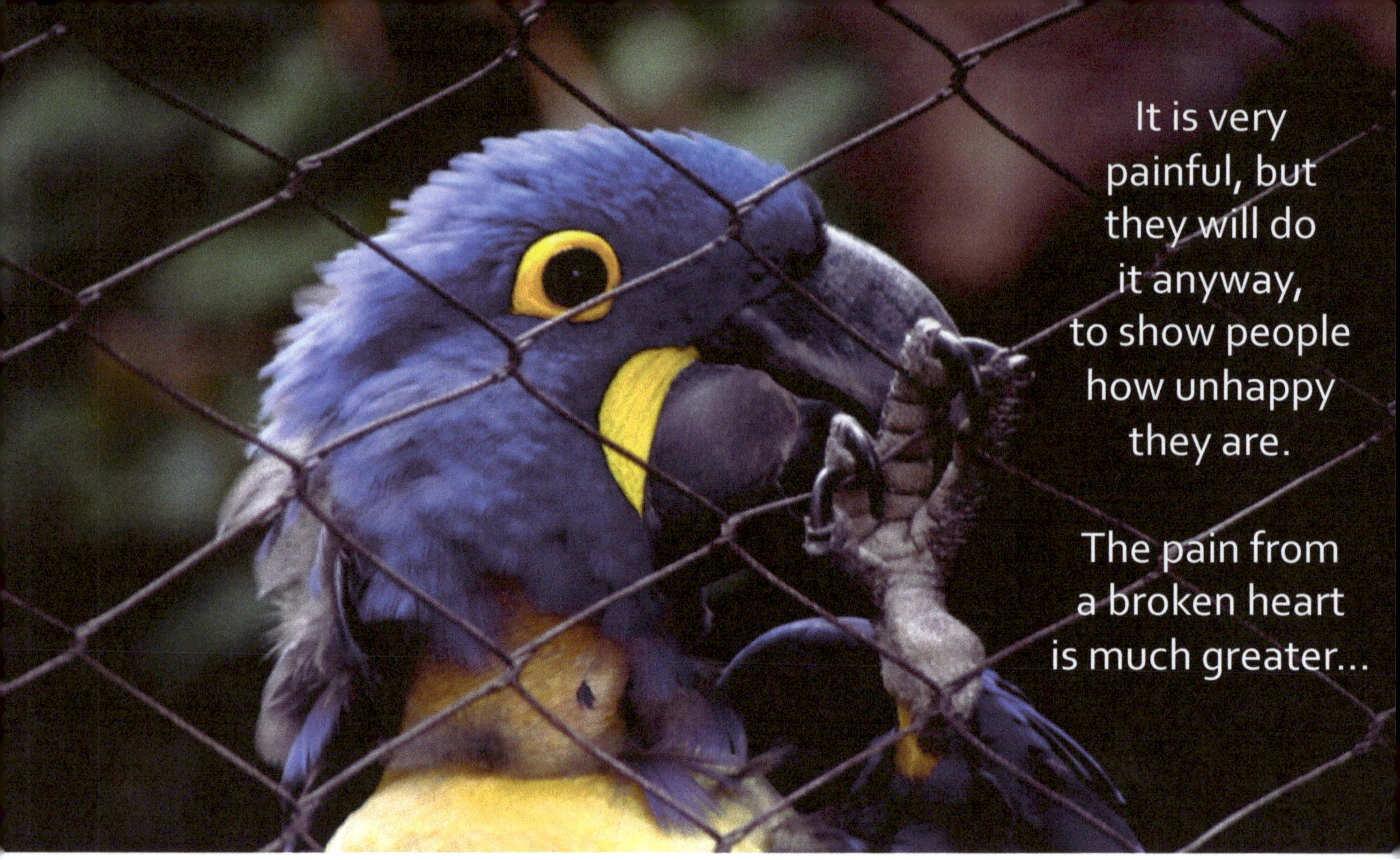

It is very
painful, but
they will do
it anyway,
to show people
how unhappy
they are.

The pain from
a broken heart
is much greater...

There are more Macaws in captivity now, than in the wild....

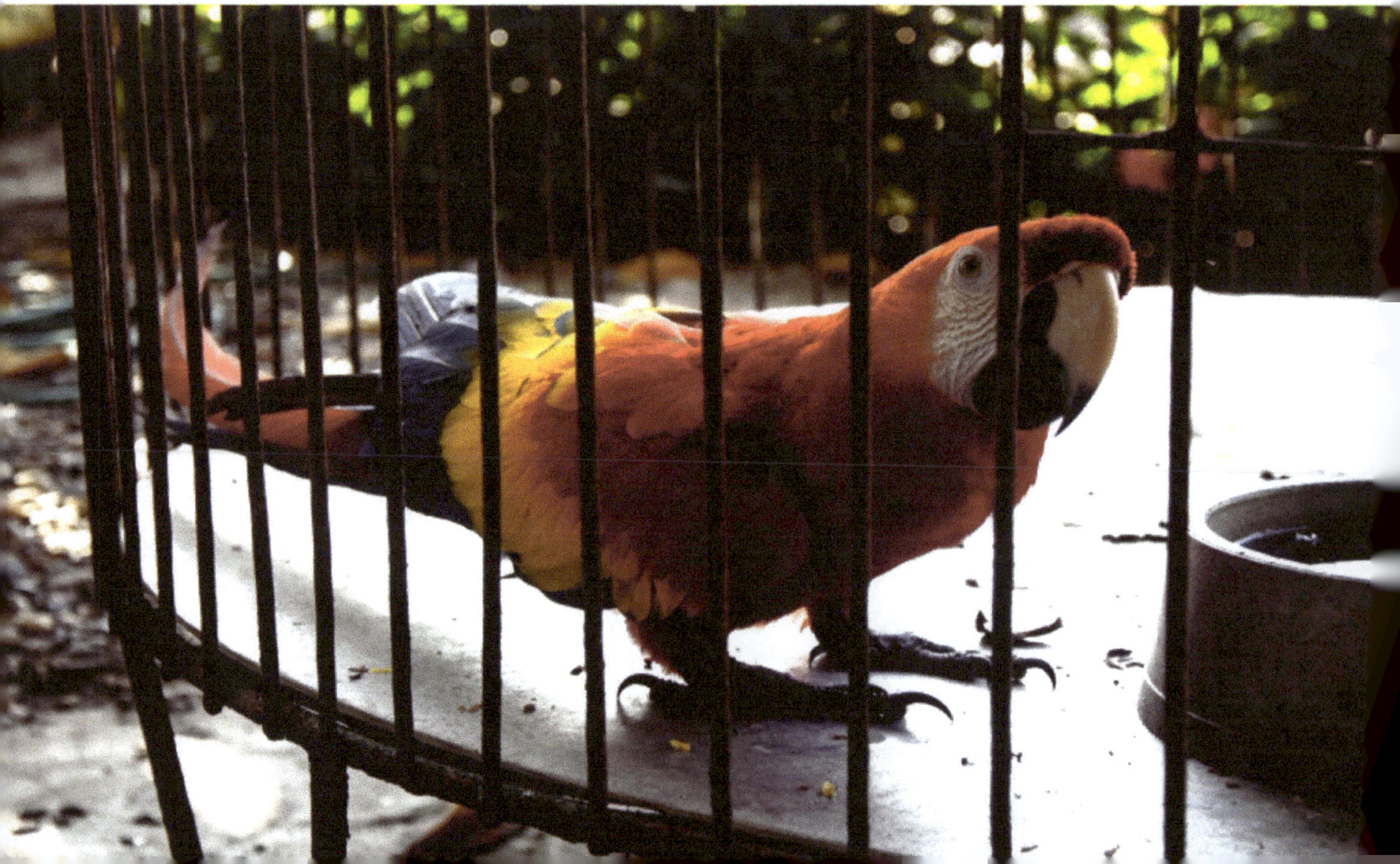

They would love to do
what we do.
Be wild and free as nature
wants them to be.

Many of us Macaws are **endangered,**
some species are already **extinct.**

(**Extinct** – The entire species has died out and no longer exists in the wild or in captivity)
(**Endangered** – Very close to extinction, only a small number of individuals left in the wild)

Glaucous macaw
(highly endangered or already extinct)
Hyacinth Macaw (probably extinct in wild)
Indigo macaw
Spix's macaw – little blue macaw
(probably extinct in the wild)
Blue – and - Yellow macaw
Blue – throated macaw
Military macaw
Great green macaw (endangered)
Scarlet macaw
Red - and - green macaw
Red – fronted macaw
Chestnut – fronted macaw
Cuban red macaw (extinct)
Saint Croix macaw (extinct)
Red – bellied macaw
Blue – headed macaw
Blue – winged macaw
Golden – collared macaw
Red – shouldered macaw

There are two main reasons for this;   **poaching**…

(**Poaching** – people illegally hunting or capturing animals from the wild)

and **deforestation** – habitat loss.

(**Deforestation** – cutting down trees, forests, to plant new crops, to build houses and roads. Damaging and destroying natural ecosystems where animals can live)

Animals natural habitat is fragmented into many small sections
by human development, such as houses
and roads, by deforestation and agriculture.

Animals find it very difficult to survive in these small,
disconnected areas.

They are either pushed out of their homes or challenged daily
by direct contact with humans.

AGRICULTURE

MINING

HUMAN DEVELOPMENT

Too many animals and plants are struggling to survive through
the destruction of the natural world caused by humans.
The list of the endangered ones is very long…

So what you can do to help us?
Love us, Learn about us, but Leave us
where we belong, in our shared home, Nature.
Protect our home, respect it and keep it clean.
It is important for you too!

3 x L

Love Learn Leave

L

LOVE

L

LEARN

L

LEAVE

Our home,

Nature.

Thank you for reading with me.
You are getting better at it every time.

See you again soon.

Draw or paint your very own Macaw.
Use all the colours you like.
Make him special and give him a name too.

The biggest challenge in life is to be yourself in a world that is trying to make you like everyone else…

The most important things in life aren't things…

The best answer for every question is Love.

Other titles from

Love Learn Leave
series coming soon...